THE REAL PRODUCT
SAFETY GUIDE

THE REAL PRODUCT SAFETY GUIDE

Reducing the Risk of Product Safety Alerts and Recalls

David L Davis

authorHOUSE®

AuthorHouse™ UK Ltd.
1663 Liberty Drive
Bloomington, IN 47403 USA
www.authorhouse.co.uk
Phone: 0800.197.4150

Published by AuthorHouse 08/21/2013

ISBN: 978-1-4918-7503-2 (sc)
ISBN: 978-1-4918-7531-5 (e)

Preface

The information in this guide will provide both large and small companies with a detailed process for ensuring that their products are inherently safe and compliant with the guidelines specified in The British Health and Safety Act of 1974.The Australian Health and Safety Act 1991.The United States Military Standard 882 and the Human Factors Engineering Standard 1472.

Everyone in business should ask themselves this question 'Would our current documentation covering our products, processes, or procedures stand up to close safety scrutiny with regard to providing documented proof and evidence of Hazard Analysis and Acceptable Risk?'

Contents

Definitions and Abbreviations

Damage   the partial or total loss of hardware caused by component failure; exposure of hardware to heat, fire or other inadvertent events or conditions.

Hazard   A condition, which could result in death, personal injury or harm and a failure of a system, plant or equipment.

Hazard Severity   An assessment of the worst credible mishap that could be caused by a specific hazard..

Hazard Probability. An assessment by an expert in the appropriate domain of how probable a mishap could occur on a specific hazard.

Safety.   Freedom from those conditions that can cause death, injury, occupational illness, or damage to, or loss of equipment.

Risk.   An expression of the severity and possibility levels associated with a specific hazard.

NASA   National Aeronautical and Space Administration.

ALARP.   As Low As Reasonably Practical.

HSE   Health and Safety Executive

Introduction

There is no such thing as one hundred percent safety because whatever action or procedure we undertake there will always be a risk. This may be caused by the interaction with a component or something else.

The things we come into contact with in life all have different forms of hazards associated to them, they could be such things as electricity, chemicals, radiation, heat, lasers, pressure, cold, water, height, food, the list is endless and I am sure the reader could easily add to this list. We cannot always remove these hazards completely from our surroundings however what we can do is reduce the chances of anyone coming to any harm.

This can be achieved by identifying all of the hazards present within a system or process and taking the necessary precautions to reduce the risk(s). If we take electricity as an example we know that the power in our home could kill if we were to receive an electric shock, so we are protected by isolation and insulation from the dangers, thus reducing the risk.

This guide explains the methodology used to achieve safety by the use of Hazard Analysis and Risk Assessment.

Every organisation requires a structured process that involves all members of its staff and culminates in a safety system second to none which results in what is commonly termed as a **Safety Culture.**

Many of our organisations do not have a comprehensive Safety Culture, which has led to many disasters that could have been prevented. We will continue to see regular disasters and nothing will change unless companies have an actual commitment to make safety the major priority by implementation and not just by words.

Chapter 1
The Law

The Health and Safety Act of 1974 is the foundation of Health and Safety in the United Kingdom, however the way organisations and agencies implement the act varies. Companies and businesses should have a member of staff who is responsible for ensuring their organisation complies with the Health and Safety law.

Health and Safety regulations are extensive and are frequently updated and amended and anyone who fails to keep abreast of the latest regulations risks a heavy fine or even a prison sentence if it is found that an accident was due to a neglect of safety law.

The penalties for failing to comply with safety are to be tightened and when introduced will make company directors more accountable and in extreme cases liable to be charged with corporate manslaughter which could result in imprisonment.

AN EXTRACT FROM THE HEALTH AND SAFETY ACT 1974.

The Health and Safety at work Act 1974 places specific duties on designers and manufacturers or articles and substances.

These are intended to ensure that only safe products are placed on the market and the following applies:—

To discover and so far as is reasonably practicable, to eliminate and minimise all risks.

To ensure, so far as is reasonably practicable that the article or substance is safe at all times.

To carry out testing and examinations to ensure that the article or substance is safe at all times.

To provide the user with information about the use of the article or substance and any conditions necessary to ensure safety.

So far as reasonably practicable, to provide the user with all revisions of information arising from the identification of new, or previously unidentified, serious hazards.

Similar procedural rules and penalties apply to offences under any of the existing statutory provisions, being offences for which no other penalty is specified. The existing statutory provisions defined by Schedule 1 of the Health and Safety Act.

In other words they consist of all the relevant statutory provisions; e.g. the Factories Act 1961, and the Explosives Act 1923, etc and regulations and orders in force before the advent of the Health and Safety Act.

Under Section 100(1) (d) of the Employment Rights Act 1996 employees who reasonably fear that they may be subjected to imminent or serious danger at work and who leave or refuse to return to work, are protected against detrimental treatment in that dismissal is deemed automatically unfair.

There is increasing pressure on the Government to make employers more accountable for the safety of their organisations.

THE SAFETY ORGANISATION.

The safety within a company normally covers two main areas, which are the Health and Safety on company sites and **Product Safety.** The Site Safety Officer will ensure that good house keeping is employed and will control such things as Subcontractors safety on site, traffic restrictions, fire precautions including fire practice and the provision and the placing of signs etc. He will also be responsible for maintaining a set of safety regulations. It will depend on how large the company is as to whether this is a full time job.

The Product Safety role is completely different and is often not understood, however it is a vital part of any safety culture and is the fundamental part of this guide.

The person who fills this position must have had a wide knowledge of the type of product base used by the company plus some experience in product safety.

PRODUCT SAFETY.

It is never too early to introduce Product Safety because the main aim is to design safety into the system from the very beginning, this means that when the costs are estimated some of the budget is allocated to the safety requirement.

The other element that is often overlooked is Human Factors Engineering that has a direct interrelationship with safety. Human Factors is exactly as the name implies and is the human machine interface that allows us to complete tasks in a natural way and at ease. There are many examples where this has not been the case in the past, the domestic cooker being one, where the oven has not always been at waist height!

Since becoming involved in the Product Safety and Human Factors field I have been alarmed by the lack of awareness of this aspect of safety, that I believe has been the major contributing factor to some of the recent disasters.

One crucial part of Product Safety is the incorporation of safe procedures into the system.

Product Safety has a structured process that is based on teamwork and involves all of the staff from the Chief Executive to the latest employee.

Once the structured process is in place a **Safety Culture** will provide a **Duty of Care** that is second to none. This guide explains the methodology and risk assessment techniques for all staff who are responsible for providing a product procedure or service.

THE HUMAN IN THE LOOP.

The first thing is to define what we mean by Safety and Human Factors Engineering, as already stated in the introduction nothing is one hundred percent safe and once we interact with an item, process, or procedure we introduce an element of risk, so if we are able to reduce the risk(s) to the lowest possible level we will have an inherently safe system.

One of the most common risks that we subject ourselves to is travel and one of the safest modes of transport is by air even though it is feared by many people. The reason it is safe is due to a Safety Culture operated by the Airlines and the Civil Aviation Authority, which is strictly adhered to, even so, things can still go wrong due to unforeseen circumstances.

Chapter 2
Safety Awareness

CASE HISTORY ONE

Some years ago a British Airways B747 departed at night from an airport in Malaysia on route with approximately four hundred passengers on board. The aircraft had an uneventful take off and climbed to the cruising altitude of around thirty three thousand feet and the cabin crew had begun the normal routine of attending to the passengers in flight requirements.

The flight crew were monitoring the airliners track along the airway when without any warning all four engines failed in a very short space of time this in turn caused most of the main systems to shut down including the pressure control system and main cabin lighting.

The oxygen masks automatically dropped down and the cabin staff were busy trying to calm everyone. The flight crew has a set of masks, which are more robust than the ones provided for passengers and resemble something, that looks more like a gas mask

The First Officer (Co pilot) had a problem with his oxygen supply so there was a high risk of him blacking out. The Captain sent out a Mayday distress message and set his secondary radar to emergency. The radio message was received at the nearest control centre which happened to be in Indonesia, unfortunately the Air Traffic Controller could not understand the message explaining all four engines had failed, this is not unusual and not the fault of the controller radio frequencies can be weak and difficult to understand at times at long range.

If we pause and assess what stress the Captain was under at this point this was a real Human Factors situation it is difficult to imagine the pressure the flight crew were under. The Captain was in a *dynamic* situation by this I mean the problems were compounded by a time element in other words every second was another second towards disaster, fortunately most professions are not *dynamic* so when a problem occurs time can be taken to solve it. If we list the problems the Captain needed to overcome in a short space of time they were daunting, A First Officer without any Oxygen and liable to black out at

5

any time, an airliner with no power and four hundred frightened passengers, no landing airport within gliding range, no idea why the engines had failed, the aircraft airspeed needing to be maintained above the stalling speed to prevent the aircraft plunging to earth, poor radio contact with Air Traffic Control.

This situation could have led to panic however it did not because of the professional competence of the crew, which I believe was enhanced by the safety culture employed by the Airline.

The safety programme, which requires flight crews to have regular training sessions in the Simulator with a varied catalogue of simulated aircraft emergency and failures; provide the aircrew with the fundamental grounding of corrective processes and procedures.

A British Airways B747

<u>Case History (Two)</u>

The Kegworth air crash was again a dynamic situation where the crisis occurred at night on a flight from London to Ireland.

The crew knew they had a problem on one of the two engines and shut down one engine and requested a diversion to their home base in the Midlands, unfortunately the aircraft crashed just short of the runway on the edge of a motorway.

It was claimed the crew shut down the wrong engine if this was the case there was probably a reason this happened. We have already considered dynamic situations where instant decisions and actions are required and in these conditions it is vital the persons concerned are given a clear indication on what has failed. In the case of aircraft instrumentation it is very important that the layout is easy to monitor due to the large display.

One report on this incident stated that one of the relevant instruments that provided information to the crew was only the size of a two pence coin.

Even though we have air disasters from time to time this is not an area we should be concerned about from a safety point of view because as stated there is a safety culture in place and unless some group decide to place profit before safety there will be no problem.

Unless a safety culture is adopted in all areas throughout society we will continue to see disasters occurring at regular intervals.

When a disaster happens the Government of the day usually declares there will be a Public Inquiry and no stone will be left unturned, however it is unfortunate the findings of some inquires tend to identify the related cause to human error in the group directly involved, which even though correct is not always the whole story and diverts attention from what was not done prior to the accident.

The authorities such as the Health and Safety Executive carry out investigations following an accident which usually results in a number of safety recommendations being implemented this only goes to prove we have failed because this corrective action indicates safety was defective in the first place. It should not take a disaster to happen before we take important safety measures.

Safety needs to be addressed at the start of every design process or procedure, this does not occur in many cases and once a system or process is in operation it becomes harder to make it safe due to the fact that the major changes are no longer a practical option. An example of this is the English Channel Tunnel Freight Rolling Stock where the Fire Service commented the design of the wagons would act like a blow torch in a fire situation, this has since been proven to be correct and the group of truck drivers involved in the Channel Tunnel fire were very fortunate to escape with their lives.

The Kegworth Disaster

CASE HISTORY (THREE)

The Herald of Free Enterprise Disaster.

The sinking of the Roll on Roll off Ferry at Zeebrugge.

Everyone was saying how could this happen something so fundamental as not closing the bow doors before this North Sea ferry departed.

The crew member responsible for normally closing the bow doors took a great deal of the blame, however the real cause was a failure to have in place safety measures that include Hazard Analysis and fail safe procedures. The disaster happened in March, 1987 and according to the Court of Inquiry the person usually responsible for closing the bow doors was the Assistant Boson who said he would often find someone else had closed them. He had been given other duties on this occasion and after being dismissed by the Boson went to his cabin, laid on his bunk and dropped off to sleep. I believe we have all experienced an instant doze at some point in our lives when our body is overtaken by fatigue in the warm surroundings. The Chief Officer was on the car deck and it was his responsibility to confirm the bow doors were closed but there was not a requirement to report anything to the bridge unless he found the bow doors open .He told the inquiry that he had asked one of the crew to close the doors but could not remember who. When Harbour Stations are called the Chief Officers position is on the bridge and it appears he went straight there without checking to see if the bow doors were closed.

If the Ferry Companies had a Safety Culture such as the Airlines the pre-departure checks would have ensured the bow doors were closed. It was fatal to rely on everything going to plan especially when a safety critical system or procedure was in operation. The crewman could have been prevented from closing the bow doors due to many other reasons, he could have been taken ill, fallen down some stairs or had a heart attack the list is endless. The Masters of some ships had previously requested that warning lights be fitted on the bridge to warn if the bow doors were open. A Director of the Company denied this until a memo was produced.

The ballast water tank at the front of the ship had not been emptied before sailing which made it easier for the water to spill over onto the car deck Due to the lack of safety procedures 188 people died.

How safety conscious are organisations when having to cope with large amounts of people? It is still the case that in many instances overcrowding takes place and can be frightening for anyone in the midst of large crowds trying to pass through a narrow space. It may be satisfactory in normal conditions for large volumes of people to queue in gangways and stairs however the situation can rapidly change if there is a fire or similar problem.

It is important that companies consider safety every time they initiate a change of any kind. We have seen a vast amount of mergers and takeovers in recent years that can have a dramatic effect on safety. When we design a ferry to operate in the open sea it will need to have the appropriate features to cope with the conditions that it will encounter. However when we have a merger of two companies and a collection of ships are used and safety is not considered we could have ships being used for something they were not designed for.

A well known ferry company merged with another shipping line some years ago and used a mix of ships on a busy channel route. The ships varied in age with the main difference being the newer ships were bigger to cope with larger amounts of passengers. At certain times during the day approximately thirty coaches are loaded plus lorries and cars. The new ferries have sixteen stairwells leading from the lower vehicle decks to the lounges and upper decks, however the older ferries only had eight stairwells. On the old ship it took passengers around fifteen minutes to climb from the base of the ship to the lounge due to the amount of passengers joining the stairwells at each deck In a fire situation there would have been no escape.

The Herald of Free Enterprise.

CASE HISTORY (FOUR)

The Challenger Shuttle Disaster.

It has been many years since this disaster happened and there have been a number of documentaries on the reasons why the shuttle exploded into millions of pieces. The evidence presented pointed to a small component called an `O` Ring as being the cause. The purpose of the `O` Ring was to flex and seal off gasses. It appears from reports that a safety culture was in place because a Hazard Analysis had identified that this component would not function correctly at low temperature. It was reported that there had been a meeting between the component subcontract manufacturer and NASA on the day before the launch and the subcontract engineers were concerned that the temperature the night before the launch was expected to drop to 28 degrees F. ·

It is unclear why the launch was allowed to go ahead because the rules of Hazard Analysis and Risk Assessment would not of allowed a launch due to an unacceptable risk caused by low temperature .The O Ring was designed to prevent exhaust leaks in

the solid rocket segments. To achieve this it needed to flex however at low temperature it was unable to do this and was classed as an acceptable risk, as long as the shuttle was not launched during periods of low temperatures.

It is vital that if a safety culture is in place the rules must always be adhered to.

The launch appeared to go according to plan at first, however after 73 seconds at 47 thousand feet the shuttle exploded into millions of pieces.

Apart from the loss of many young lives that included two women the disaster cost NASA so much it is difficult to measure, not only was there a financial penalty but the whole Shuttle programme was placed in jeopardy at the time.

The Challenger Shuttle Exploding

THE COMMERCIAL PRESSURES.

With the commercial pressures of today there must be many companies who are tempted to take undesirable risks, which is not a good idea, apart from putting peoples lives at risk it can be very damaging for any organisation large or small.

It is not always a deliberate policy to deceive in some cases a failure in design with regard to safety can cause a problem as one very famous German car manufacturer discovered.

After the car had been built it was found that it was unstable and prone to tipping over on tight cornering. The corrective measures, which had to be implemented, and all the unfavourable publicity cost the company many millions of pounds.

It makes sense for all organisations to spend money at the design and development stage of any project or venture because if it is left and addressed at the time of delivery it is too late and any changes tend to be cosmetic, which is not suggesting that nothing should be done in this situation.

It is unfortunate that some companies do just the minimum with regards to safety just to stay within the law. Safety should be seen as an investment because if a complete Hazard Analysis is not initiated at the start and a disaster occurs at a later point the additional money required for the safety measures will pale into insignificance compared with the compensation and loss of business due to a public lack of confidence.

SOFTWARE.

There are many systems, which rely on software, and when companies are trying to win contracts there is a great temptation to cut cost by reducing software-testing time to a minimum.

I have yet to see estimated software time scales meeting their targets that is not a bad situation if it means they operate correctly at the end of the day.

If a Hazard Analysis is not completed where Safety Critical Software is present there will be major consequences (Safety Critical Software is a state where a system is controlled by software and can cause a life threatening situation if the software fails to operate the system in the way it is designed.)

It is becoming more difficult to control safety due to the purchasing of items off the shelf and the closing down of manufacturing.

Chapter 3
A Step by Step Guide to Real Safety

The first thing to establish is who does what.

The Safety Specialist / Safety Officer /Safety Engineer /Safety Consultant./ Safety Authority.

A safety person can have any of the above titles but this does not mean he or she will make a product safe by completing a safety analysis of the product or system.

The role of the safety person is to ensure a structured process is in place and the experts in each area concerned correctly and comprehensively analyse the hazards and risks.

A basic structured process contains at least the following documents:—

System Safety Programme Plan.
Preliminary Hazard Analysis.
Final Hazard Analysis.
Audit Report.
Safety Certification.
Human Factors Engineering Programme Plan.
Human Factors System Analysis.
Human Factors Critical Task Analysis.
Hazard Operability Study (HAZOP)

The writing of the System Safety Programme Plan is one of the first tasks the safety specialist is required to undertake and before this is attempted the company safety organisation must be established.

THE SYSTEM SAFETY PROGRAMME PLAN.

The first step an organisation or company needs to do is write a System Safety Programme Plan .The information in this plan will explain how the safety data is organised and who is responsible for each part, this is very important because if we are to analyse each part of the system we need to know the boundaries and at what point it becomes the responsibility of someone else. In the larger projects there may be a number of companies involved in the one system and therefore it is vital everyone understands which areas they are responsible and accountable for.

The System Safety Programme Plan is required to be a guide to all staff working on the project so they have no doubt what they have to do and how they shall present the documentation.

A typical System Safety Plan will contain the following ten sections with section six being further sub-divided into four stages.

SYSTEM SAFETY PROGRAMME PLAN TABLE OF CONTENTS.

Section 1   Scope (complete project) *Short description of who is involved.*

Section 2   Introduction *Synopsis that describes the project.*

Section 3   Reference Documents *Relevant Standards, and Company Procedures.*

Section 4   Scope (your company) *The part(s) your company is responsible for.*

Section 5   Safety Organisation *Show chart of family tree*

Section 6   Safe Design Plan. *The stages of safety in design.*

Section 7   Hazard Analysis Check Lists

Section 8   Product Item Equipment Configurations

Section 9   Attachments

Section 10   Design Approval and Design Certification.

The following gives an example of each section of the System Safety Programme Plan. These are only examples and need to be expanded into the actual project being implemented.

Section 1 (Example)

Scope

This System Safety Programme Plan is produced in accordance with . . . . and satisfies the requirements of . . . . standard, subcontract agreement, ... Task . . . .

The document describes the system safety programme to be undertaken by . . . . and the methodology and organisation in place.

Section 2 (Example)

Introduction.

System Safety forming part of the . . . . scope for the . . . . contract requires the co-ordination and interrelationship of all internal and external areas involved in Design, Production, Software, Hardware etc.

The purpose of the document is to establish a formal safety programme plan covering the life of the project with the aim of achieving the highest possible level of safety, early hazard identification and elimination plus a reduction of associated risk.

A point acceptable to the Managing activity and is the principle contribution of effective system safety.

Section 3 (Example)

Reference Documents.

List Safety Documents
List Standards.

BS6656   Inadvertent ignition of flammable atmospheres by
                                    radio Frequency radiation.

BS6657   Prevention of inadvertent initiation of electro
                                    explosive devices by radio frequency radiation.

Section 4 (Example)

Scope.

*Those requirements for which you are responsible as listed in the Requirements
Specification.*

Task
101   (1)   System Safety Programme Plan.

102   (2)   Integration Management of Subcontractors.

103   (3)   System Safety Programme Reviews.

105   (4)   Hazard Tracking and Risk Resolution.

106   (5)   Test and Evaluation Safety.

107   (6)   System Safety Progress Summary.

108   (7)   Qualifications of Key System Safety Personnel.

201   (8)   Preliminary Hazard List (PHL).

202   (9)   Preliminary Hazard Analysis (PHA).

203   (10)   *System Hazard Analysis.*

205   (11)   *Operating and Support Hazard Analysis.*

206   (12)   *Occupational Health Hazard Assessment (OHHA).*

207   (13)   *Safety Verification.*

209   (14)   *Safety Assessment Report.*

210   (15)   *Safety Compliance Assessment*

211   (16)   *Safety Reviews Changes and Waivers.*

301   (17)   *Software Requirements Hazard Analysis (SRHA).*

302   (18)   *Top Level Design Hazard Analysis.*

303   (19)   *Detailed Design Hazard Analysis.*

304   (20)   *Code Level Software Hazard Analysis.*

305   (21)   *Software Safety Testing.*

306   (22)   *Software User Interface Analysis.*

307   (23)   *Software Change Hazard Analysis*

        (24)   *Commercial Off The Shelf COTS Hazard Analysis.*

Task 101   System Safety Programme Plan.

The purpose of Task 101 is to develop a System Safety Plan. It shall describe in detail tasks and activities of system safety management and system safety engineering required to identify evaluate and eliminate hazards or reduce the associated risk to a level acceptable to the Managing Activity (MA). (The Managing Activity are those responsible at each stage of the process.)

Task 102   Integration Management of Associated Contractors.

The purpose of Task 102 is to provide the system integrating Contractor and MA with appropriate management surveillance of other contractors system safety progress.

Task 103   System Safety Programme Reviews.

The purpose of Task 103 is to establish a requirement for the contractor to present system safety programme reviews and to periodically report the status of the system safety programme.

Task 105   Hazard Tracking and Risk Resolution.

The purpose of Task 105 is to establish a single close loop hazard Tracking system.

Task 106   Test and Evaluation Safety.

The purpose of Task 106 is to make sure safety is considered in Test and Evaluation, to provide existing analysis reports and other safety data.

Task 107   System Safety Progress Summary.

The purpose of Task 107 is to provide a periodic progress report summarising the pertinent system safety management and engineering activity that occurred during the reporting period.

Task 108   Qualifications of Key System Safety Personnel.

The purpose of Task 108 is to establish qualifications for key contractor system safety engineers and managers.

Task 201   Preliminary Hazard List.

The purpose of Task 201 is to compile a preliminary hazard list (PHL) very early in the system acquisition life cycle to enable the MA to choose any hazardous areas on which to put management emphasis.

Task 202   Preliminary Hazard Analysis

The purpose of Task 202 is to perform and document a preliminary hazard analysis (PHA) to identify safety critical areas, evaluate hazards, and identify the safety design criteria to be used.

Task 203   System Hazard Analysis.

The purpose of Task 203 is to perform and document a system hazard analysis to identify hazards associated with design of subsystems including component failure modes, critical human error inputs, and hazards resulting from functional relationships between components and equipment comprising each subsystem.

Task 205   Operating and Support Hazard Analysis.

The purpose of Task 205 is to perform and document an operating and support hazard analysis to identify hazards and recommend risk reduction alternatives during all phases of intended system use. This process is normally required at an installation site where there are different phases that present changing hazards, for example phase one maybe the demolition of a building and phase two could be the moving in of heavy equipment involving different hazards. This Task is linked TASK 106.

Task 206   Occupational Health Hazard Assessment.

The purpose of Task 206 is to perform and document an occupational health hazard assessment (OHHA) to identify health hazards and propose protective measures to reduce the associated risk to a level acceptable to the Managing Activity.(MA)

Task 207   Safety Verification.

The purpose of Task 207 is to define and perform tests and demonstrations or use other verification methods on safety critical hardware, software, and procedures to verify compliance with safety requirements.

Task 209   Safety Assessment Report.

The purpose of Task 209 is to perform and document a comprehensive evaluation of the mishap risks being assumed prior to test or operation of a system or at contract completion.

Task 210   Safety Compliance Assessment.

The purpose of Task 210 is to perform and document a safety compliance assessment to verify compliance with military, national, and industry codes imposed contractually or by law to ensure safe design of a system.

Task 211   Safety Reviews of Change proposals and Waivers.

The purpose of Task 211 is to perform and document analyses of Engineering change proposals and requests for waiver to determine the Safety impact on the system.

Task 301   Software Requirements Hazard Analysis.

The purpose of Task 301 is to require the contractor to perform and document a Software Requirements Hazard Analysis (SRHA). The contractor shall examine system and software requirements and design In order to identify unsafe modes for resolution, such as out-of-sequence, wrong event, inappropriate magnitude, inadvertent command, adverse environment, deadlocking, failure to command modes etc.

Task 302   Top Level Design Hazard Analysis.

The purpose of Task 302 is to require the contractor to perform and document a Top-Level Design Hazard Analysis. The contractor shall analyse the Top Level Design using the results of the SRHA Task 301 if previously accomplished.

Task 303   Detailed Design Hazard Analysis.

The purpose of Task 303 is to require the contractor to perform and document a Detailed Design Hazard Analysis .The contractor shall analyse the Software Detailed Design, using the results of SRHA Task 301 and Task 302to verify the correct incorporation of safety requirements and to analyse the safety critical computer software components. This analysis shall be substantially complete before coding of the software is started.

Task 304   Code Level Software Hazard Analysis.

The purpose of Task 304 is to require the contractor to perform and document a Code-Level Software Hazard Analysis. Using the results Task 303 the contractor shall analyse programme code and system interfaces for events, faults, and conditions which could cause or contribute to undesired events affecting safety. The analysis shall start when coding begins and continue throughout the system life cycle.

Task 305   Software Safety Testing.

The purpose of Task 305 is to require the contractor to perform and document Safety Testing.

Task 306   Software User Interface Analysis.

The purpose of Task 306 is as follows:- Provide for the detection of a hazard condition. Provide for a safe survival and recovery methodology from a detected Critical hazard condition. Incorporate an operator-warning feature to alert the operator of\ software errors that result in the non conformance of equipment malfunctions.

Task 307   Software Change Hazard Analysis.

All changes to specifications, requirements, design, code, systems, equipment, and test plans, descriptions, procedures, cases, or criteria shall be subjected to software hazard analysis and testing, unless it can be shown to be unnecessary due to the nature of the change. The beginning point of this change hazard analysis shall be the highest within the documentation or system that is affected by the change being proposed.

The above Tasks will not all be required in a normal contract only a selected number that are pertinent to the safety requirement.

Commercial Off The Shelf. (COTS).

Bought in components and equipment need to show evidence that they meet the levels of safety that will not compromise the safety of the user or the overall system. There is no point in completing a Hazard analysis on your own system and ignoring the safety risks from items purchased elsewhere

Safety documentation should obtained from the suppliers before an order is placed.

The customer will normally place a list of safety requirements in addition to the main list of requirements.

Typical Safety Requirements (Example only)

The System Safety Programme shall satisfy the safety requirements specified.

The installation shall be designed to be inherently safe with suitable screening, protective measures and physical clearances to enhance personnel safety in accordance with Standard . . . .

Where construction, installation, maintenance or operation create a hazardous environment warning shall be provided in accordance with Standard . . . .

Hazardous items shall be labelled to warn personnel of the safety hazards involved in accordance with Standard . . . .

Mechanical Hazards such as sharp projections and overhanging edges or protrusions shall be avoided.

Dangerous materials shall be stored, transported, and installed in a manner that will preclude injury to personnel or damage to the equipment.

Any substance that contains Organophosphate shall not be used.

Section 5

Safety Organisation and Responsibilities.

Policy for safety. (Example)

This section explains the company policy for safety

Responsibilities

<u>Safety Executives</u>
Safety Executives shall be appointed to direct the implementation of the safety policy and establish the functional arrangements necessary.

Their responsibilities shall include the following:-

To produce a policy statement for each safety field relevant to the area of responsibility.

To appoint personnel to perform functional safety duties as required by the relevant policy statement.

To advise those responsible for safety of any new safety appointment.

To implement a Directive regarding notification of serious accidents.

<u>Line Management.</u>
Line management shall be responsible for the following:-

To implement all requirements to meet the safety policy.

To provide for resources in the area of responsibility.

To ensure all subordinate levels of management recognise their responsibility for safety achievement.

The responsibility of all personnel is:

To comply with all instructions, procedures and disciplines relating to safety.

To report any aspect which may adversely affect the achievement of safety.

To ensure that a safe system is achieved and legal and contractual commitments are met. The fulfilling of the safety policy requires the involvement of all personnel, in other words a (**Safety Culture.**)

Duties.

Corporate/Line Management shall identify and provide. Financial Resources, Manpower, Facilities and Training.

Project Management Personnel shall promulgate and implement contract requirements.

Design and Development Personnel shall identify and minimise risks by means of Hazard Analysis, Review, Design and Labelling.

Delineation Personnel (Draughting) shall ensure data drawings specifications clearly identify risk areas and prescribe appropriate procedures to minimise risk.

Materials Management Personnel shall operate to handling and storage instructions and advise of any inadequacy.

Procurement Personnel shall ensure vendors and subcontractors are made aware of any risk areas arising from specifications and drawings. Ensure that items received comply with all specified requirements of safety. Ensure data from vendors and subcontractors is passed to the nominated area.

Manufacturing Personnel shall operate to instructions and advise of any considered inadequacy.

Packaging and Transportation Personnel shall operate to instructions especially regarding marking, handling, and precautions, plus the control and use of transport and transit vehicles / devices and advise of any considered inadequacy.

Installation Personnel shall operate to instructions and advise of any considered inadequacy.

Training Personnel shall provide all training requirements as identified by Line Management.

Repair and Refurbishing Personnel identify and report any safety aspects relevant to the repair and refurbishing.

Software Personnel shall identify and minimise risks by Hazard Operability Studies, Reviews, Design, and instruction. Ensuring any Safety Critical Software is identified.

Handbook Personnel shall ensure information provided to the customer is presented in such a manner as to clearly show correct usage including proper disposal arrangements where necessary.

Integration and Test Personnel shall ensure that the equipment or system functions in the way it is designed.

**Typical
Safety Organisation Chart.**

Managing Director

Engineering Director

Safety Authority

Product Safety Engineer

Design Authority

Design Engineers

Subcontractors

**System Safety Programme Plan
Section 6**

<u>Safety Process Design Plan.</u>

The safety process should divide the equipment or system into manageable chunks which we will call **Work Package Areas (WPAs)** there can be as many WPAs as required. If we were designing a car for example we could divide it up into twenty small chunks depending on how many design teams there are. Some design areas could be a smaller group who are part of a larger team. One Work Package Area could be responsible for the design of the cars instrumentation so the design team in this area would complete all of the safety requirements relating to instrumentation We need to identify the expert designers at the lowest defined point of the design.

The designers in each Work Package Area are responsible for completing a Hazard Analysis on the part they are designing.

The design teams document a structured process that ensures the end product is inherently safe, they are guided by a comprehensive Safety Plan that explains what is required and how each step is achieved.

There are four main stages in the Design Plan which are as follows:-

Stage One Hazard Analysis	Stage Two	Stage Three	Stage Four
	Update **Design Review**	Update	Update
		Update **Design**	Update
		Proving Safety	Update
			Audit

Stage One.

Hazard Analysis.

A Hazard Analysis for each item of equipment should be initiated during the early stage of the design process once the requirements have been agreed.

The proposed design is examined by the designers(s) (WPA) responsible for each item and all potential safety hazards, using checklists.

The risk level is also assessed in each case. The Design Authority must find ways of reducing risks to an acceptable level taking advice as appropriate.

It is vital that the high level requirements are flowed down into the low level requirements .To give an example of what is meant by high level requirements if we were designing a tractor one high level requirement might be. The tractor shall be capable of operating during the day or night. In order to satisfy this requirement there will be many lower level requirements such as the amount and type of lights needed.

If the lower level requirements have not correctly been identified major design errors can occur because the designer will be guessing what the customer requires

It is important that the safety requirements are initiated at high level so that when the lower level design is started all of the safety requirements are incorporated.

There is no point in designing equipment that will result in problems at a later point when installation or maintenance occurs.

Hazard Analysis is the most important part of any safety process and if carried out correctly will ensure that an inherently safe system will be in place.

Hazards are assessed using two main elements **Severity and Probability**. However the first task is to identify all of the hazards throughout the equipment or system and the best way of doing this is to use the expertise of a specialist in each domain or Work Package Area (WPA)

It is always a concern at the end of any safety analysis that nothing has been overlooked or forgotten.

To help in the identification of hazards it is a good idea to provide a series of checklists to use as thought provoking tools. Check lists can be made user friendly by starting at a Primary level with just the main headings requiring the person conducting the analysis to only consider those areas relevant to his or her equipment or system.

This prevents reading unnecessary checklist items.

An example of a Primary Checklist is as follows-

System safety Programme Plan.
Section 7

Primary Check List.

Check the following items on the list below and place a tick against each item that is relevant to the equipment or system being analysed.

On completion of this form go to the Secondary Check List(s) that have the same title as the ones ticked on this list.

Note: each equipment must have its own unique checklist.

Toxic Substances
Machinery
Lifting
Handling
Electrical
Explosive
Buildings,Cabins,Vehicles.
Software and Automatic Systems
Operational Systems
Temperature
Pressure Vessels
Light and Lasers
Noise
Masts and Towers
Radiation
Fire
Work Sites
Corrosion
Electro Magnetic Compatibility / Electro Magnetic Interference EMC / EMI.
Waste Disposal.

Note.
This list is intended to be thought provoking and other subjects can added as required

<u>Secondary Check List.</u>

Dangers   *Precautionary Measures*

TOXIC SUBSTANCES.

Beryllium Oxide   *Danger to personnel if broken particles are*
                                         inhaled or come into contact with cuts or
                                         abrasions.

                                         Heating to decomposition causes highly
                                         Dangerous fumes to be given off.
P.T.F.E.   *Decomposes at approximately 300 degrees C*
Poly tetra fluoro ethylene   *giving off hazardous fumes.*

Insulation Plastics (PVC)   *Gives off highly toxic fumes when ignited .*

Asbestos   *Dust and fibres very hazardous if inhaled*
                                         Must be strictly controlled by experts.
                                         Replacement and repair of lagging made of this
                                         material can be hazardous.
                                         Use alternative materials.

Mineral Oils   *Can cause Skin Cancer / Scrotal Cancer.*

Lead   *Toxic by inhalation or ingestion.*
                                         Beware of contamination to hands.
                                         When melted will produce toxic fumes.

Magnesium   *Machining, filing, or abrading will produce a*
                                         high fire risk from the swarf and dust produced.

Mercury   *Toxic fumes given off at room temperature.*
                                         Contaminated hands can lead to ingestion.

Cadmium   *Red heat produces highly toxic fumes.*

Corrosion   *causes white rust which is a Highly toxic dust.*

Various Solvents

Some are flammable.
Some are toxic.
Some can cause Narcosis.
Always check data sheets before use and if in doubt call the manufacturer.

MACHINERY.

Trapping — *Use protective covers screens or fences*

Cutting — *Use protective covers and screens.*

Entanglement — *Control and use of correct clothing, rings etc.*

Crushing — *Use of sirens, alarms, fences, warning signs.*

Striking — *Use of sirens, alarms, fences, interlocks, warning signs*

Nipping — *Covers.*

LIFTING.

Mechanical

Items that weigh over 40 kg should be lifted using a Mechanical aid.

Mechanical lifting equipment and associated items must be regularly inspected in accordance with Health and Safety regulations and must have the relevant Safety Certification.

Only trained personnel are permitted to operate Equipment and use slings.

Lifting equipment failure can lead to damage or injury

Poor design can cause difficulties of access or attachment leading to misuse.

Misuse can cause damage by abrasion or impact.

Regularly check for signs of corrosion.

Human Lift

Reduce weight when possible by dismantling equipment into smaller units.

Females are employed in some jobs that require some lifting. The safe weight for a female lift is lower than a male.

The safe maximum weight for a one female lift is 16.8 kg.

The safe maximum weight for a one male lift is 20 kg.

If two people are used i.e. two females or two males the weight quoted above can be doubled.

To prevent back injury it is important that personnel are trained how to lift items correctly.

HANDLING

Manual lifting of heavy items.
Provide training.
Provide sufficient handles and lifting points in the correct position to ensure stability.
Do not place heavy items in high locations.

Inadequate lifting points.
Always use trained personnel especially when using slings.

Safety involving Mechanical
Provide separate walkways from routes and Pathways used to move heavy items.

Cranes and Fork Lift Trucks
Have the appropriate equipment and trained Staff to off load deliveries.

ELECTRICAL.

Dangerous High Voltages
present in Equipment
(30VAC) (50VDC)

Design to restrict access incorporate Covers and interlocks.
Instructions.
Reduction of risk during access.
Isolation precautions Earth frames, panels, and connectors.

Dangerous Voltages present
after Switch off.

Design to quench voltage (earth switch) Design to restrict access.
Reduce risk during access
Warning signs
Provide discharge probe

Control of high voltage
or high power in a
mis-operation or fault
situation.

Calculate and evaluate the effects of possible mis-operation and fault condition. Provide fusing protection circuits.
Security of fault paths.

TEMPERATURE.

Consequence of contact
burning scalding.

Measurement and calculation during normal operation and conditions.
Design to reduce risk by incorporating covers, screening, insulation and fencing Over and under temperature trip.
Selection of materials.
Warning notices.
Protective clothing.

Hot or cold conditions.

Ensure adequate ventilation.
Include fans to reduce temperature.
Forced blown air.

Consequence of
decomposition or melting of
substances.

Toxic fumes and fire precautions.

PRESSURE VESSELS.

Explosion or rupture due to inadequate design, faulty manufacture, misuse, or fault condition.

Selection and assessment of materials.
Stress analysis.
Consideration of environmental conditions.

Fitting relief valves, pressure gauges,
Choice of fittings to prevent confusion of supplies.
Warning notices.
Maintenance instructions.
Inspection.
Test and Certification.
Working pressure labels.
Calibration of gauges.

LIGHT AND LASERS.

Light

Design to reduce risk.

Glare

Measurement and assessment of light.

Rhythmic flicker causing Epileptic fits

Diffusion and or shielding.

Intense light.

Lasers

Design to reduce risk.
Use alternative methods as light source where possible Light emitting diode (LED)
Shielding
Warnings and Instructions
Labels
Class
Lasers can cause severe damage to the eyes.

NOISE.

Reduction or impairment of hearing	*Reduce risk by design.*
	Place noise budget requirements on Room equipment suppliers.
	Measurement and evaluation.
Disturbance of personnel involved In communications leading to Impairment of efficiency.	*Enclosure*
	Warnings
	Personal headphones.
	Baffling
	Ear defenders
Inability to hear speech or warnings.	*Limited access.*

MASTS AND TOWERS.

Instability	*Design to reduce risk*
	Assessment of materials
Earth movement	*Stress analysis.*
	Assessment of geological conditions
Damage by impact	*Beacons*
	Choice of location
	Fencing to prevent unauthorised entry.
Environmental conditions	*Light walkways*
Rescue of personnel.	*Provide hand holds*
Fitting of equipment	*Lifting facilities*
Adverse weather	*Permit to work*
Problems of access	*Non slip materials*
Unauthorised climbing	*Plate base of ladders*
Taking tools aloft	*Provide anchorage points for safety belt*
	Supply toe boards
Lighting	*Non slip materials*
Lightning	*Lightning conductors..*

Provide comprehensive instructions.

FIRE.

Ignition of materials.	*Design to reduce risk.*
Ignition of flammable liquids	*Use non combustible materials.*
Persons trapped or injured by fire.	*Separate heat sources.*
Inadequate fire precautions	*Provide fire alarms.*
No escape route / Fire escape.	*Provide training and drills.*
No fire doors / ventilation causing spread of fire.	*Provide fire fighting equipment.*
	Provide emergency lighting.
	Provide escape routes plus signs.
	Provide fire escapes.
	Provide off switch for ventilation.
	Ensure good house keeping is carried out.

For a fire to burn it requires three main elements

HEAT
OXYGEN
MATERIAL

Remove one or more of these elements and the fire will extinguish.

Ensure staff are trained in the correct use of fire appliances, obtain expert advice on fire fighting equipment from the Fire Service.

Water is a good conductor of electricity and shall not be used on fires where electricity is present. Chemical, Oil, and Gas fires also require special methods and treatment.

WORK SITES.

Structural Hazards.	*Examine for obstructions or holes on the floor of working area.*
	Ensure adequate lighting.
Part Installation Hazards.	*Ensure floors can support weight of equipment and or materials.*
	Ensure electrical equipment is screened isolated and earthed.
Emergency Hazards.	*Provide personnel with instructions and warning of all hazards.*
	Ensure personnel wear the correct safety clothing including hard hat.
	Ensure emergency alarms and communications are in working order.
	Fence area from unauthorised personnel.
	Restrict access.
	Ensure a Hazard Analysis has been completed and all corrective actions are complete before work is allowed to begin.

PACKING.

Danger to user if items are incorrectly packed.	*Always use trained staff.*
	Provide warnings and instructions.
Deterioration due to extended storage in adverse conditions.	*Ensure contents are protected from any outside elements such as water and excessive heat.*
Damage to product due to hazardous materials.	
Danger to public due to hazardous materials.	*Transport hazardous materials using the least risk to the public.*

Inadequate containers.

Display weight of item and provide the appropriate handling aids.

Sling points forklift pallets, Handles, etc.

CORROSION.

Failure of structure

Protect against corrosion

Test soil at site.

Failure of mechanical operation.

Test for chemical reaction.

Failure of electrical supplies.

Inspect regularly for corrosion

Provide instructions and warnings.

Note:

Some structures that have been in use for a long period of time may contain cadmium which is a harmful substance when corrosion is present. When cadmium is present personnel must receive expert advice before starting work on the structure. (see also Toxic Substances.)

SOFTWARE AND AUTOMATIC SYSTEMS.

Initiation of mechanical movement which could cause Injury i.e. striking, trapping, etc

*Complete Hazard Analysis using **HAZOP***

Initiation of electrical changes which could cause danger to persons by shock or radiation.

Out of sequence operation of equipment.

Malfunction of equipment.

Provision of wrong information.

Interaction with other equipment.

OPERATIONAL SYSTEMS.

Implications of wrong data

Loss of data.

Complete HAZOP

Loss of display device.

Confusion between training and operational status.

RADIATION.

Ionising Radiation.

X-Ray generation in high voltage equipment
Radiation from Radio nuclides
(radio active sources)
Breakage or spillage.
In the event of fire or explosion.

Non Ionising Radiation.

RF Radiation
Personnel Health.
Ignition of flammable substances and explosives.

Radiation is a specialist subject always seek advice from an expert in this field.

OTHER HAZARDS

Electromagnetic Compatibility/ Electromagnetic Interference EMC / EMI

When using electrical equipment it is important that the designer considers EMC/EMI and screens the equipment. Interference between devices can cause dangerous situations unless precautions are implemented, interference from an electric trains electrical system can result in causing a signal to operate incorrectly.

The interference can occur at any time or place as some builders who had a lucky escape discovered, when the foreman operated his mobile telephone and watched in horror as his actions caused a high rise crane to drop its heavy load, with no action being taken by the crane operator.

This is a specialist subject and the relevant experts should be consulted on the methods to achieve EMC/EMI.

If EMC / EMI is not considered until the component is complete it can cause problems with space due to the adding of additional enclosures and mesh screening..

There are a number of Test Houses throughout the country that have the appropriate Anechoic Chambers which will test equipment and provide data to enable compliance with EU Directives.

It should be remembered that companies that export electrical equipment must have the relevant paperwork for EMC/EMI to support the CE marking.

Chapter 4
Design Teams (Work Package Area)

There should be one or two Design Authorities that are in overall control of the whole system design and who report to the Project Manager. Below the Design Authorities there should be small design teams who have a team leader, these teams are termed Work Package Areas (WPAs) Each WPA would have been asked to complete a Hazard Analysis on there design using the checklists shown on the previous pages and they should have been able to identify a number of different hazards.

The next step after establishing what hazards are present is to complete a Risk Assessment which means each hazard has to be assessed for severity and probability of occurrence

Hazard Risk Assessment (HRA).

SEVERITY.

When the designer makes his assessment of severity it is based on four main levels. He needs to ask himself could this hazard cause (1) Death. (2) Serious Injury. (3) Marginal Injury or (4) Minor Injury and whatever conclusion is reached will provide a figure 1,2,3, or 4 that indicates the severity of the hazard. Remember that it is not just the designer who assesses this, the rest of the design team, the team leader and the Design Authority must also agreed that the assessment is correct.

PROBABILITY OF OCCURRENCE.

The designer must also assess the chances and frequency of this hazard occurring and causing an accident. This is separated into five main levels (A) Frequent, (B) Probable, (C) Occasional, (D) Remote, and (E) Improbable.

The designer has used his expertise to provide us with a Risk Assessment of a figure and a letter so for example an electrical appliance could have a hazard that includes high voltage such as 240v AC. Could this kill a person? The answer is `yes` so the severity is going to be (1). Have we taken any precautions to prevent anyone from being electrocuted ? The answer is `no` so the probability of occurrence will equal (A) Frequent giving a Hazard Risk Index (HRI) 1A

It is obvious we cannot have a situation where a hazard has a Risk of 1A so the answer is to take measure to reduce the probability to a lower level that will make it safe and acceptable. Please note we are only changing the probability in this example and not the severity. This is because nothing can be done about the severity in this case because we cannot lower the 240v to a safe level that would not cause death or serious injury, this is not always the case in other hazards that do not involve a standard voltage we therefore have the choice of using other options.

The example probability level of (A) can be made acceptable by reducing the risk from Frequent to Improbable (E). This is done by ensuring that safety actions are implemented on the component such as insulation, isolation, fusing, and what ever is required to protect the user from the 240volts.

The anticipated consequences of hazardous events may be **minimal** in some cases and **catastrophic** in others.

Safety Hazards are categorised into levels of acceptability based on how serious a potential hazard could be and how likely it is to occur.

The terminology for the four levels of severity that represent Death, Serious Injury, Marginal Injury, and Minor Injury are as follows:-

(!) Death   **Catastrophic.**
(2) Serious Injury   **Critical.**
(3) Marginal Injury   **Marginal.**
(4) Minor Injury   **Negligible.**

The Risk Acceptability Chart overleaf shows the levels that are acceptable.

It should be noted that when an assessment is made the worst case scenario should be assumed.

The amount of components in the system must also be considered the more components in the system the more frequent the occurrence.

David L Davis

HAZARD RISK ASSESSMENT EXAMPLE

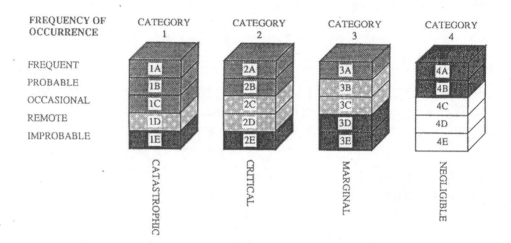

FREQUENCY OF OCCURRENCE

	CATEGORY 1	CATEGORY 2	CATEGORY 3	CATEGORY 4
FREQUENT	1A	2A	3A	4A
PROBABLE	1B	2B	3B	4B
OCCASIONAL	1C	2C	3C	4C
REMOTE	1D	2D	3D	4D
IMPROBABLE	1E	2E	3E	4E
	CATASTROPHIC	CRITICAL	MARGINAL	NEGLIGIBLE

HAZARD RISK INDEX

CRITERIA

Unacceptable

Undesirable (MA decision required)

Acceptable with review by MA

Acceptable without review

MA : Managing Activity

Definition of Terms. (Severity)

Description	Category	Definition
CATASTROPHIC	1	A hazard which could result in a situation involving death or a terminal illness, or complete loss of system availability such that the system is unable to perform its critical functions.
CRITICAL	2	A hazard which could result in a situation involving severe injury or occupational illness (e.g. injuries or illnesses that have a lasting effect.) A high probability of major system Damage.
MARGINAL	3	A hazard which could result in a situation involving minor injury or occupational illness. With low probability of minor system Availability.
NEGLIGIBLE	4	A hazard which could result in a situation involving a trivial injury or occupational illness (Scratches minor cuts etc) Minimal loss of non critical system Functions.

Definition of Terms (Probability of Occurrence.)

Description	Level	Individual Item.	Complete System.
FREQUENT	A	Likely to occur frequently	Continuously experienced
PROBABLE	B	Will occur several times.	Will occur frequently in life of item.
OCCASIONAL	C	Likely to occur at sometime.	Will occur several times in the life of an item.
REMOTE	D	Unlikely but possible to occur in the life of item.	Unlikely but can reasonably be expected to occur
IMPROBABLE	E	So unlikely it can be assumed may not be experienced.	Unlikely to occur but possible.

Note

The frequency of occurrence will depend on the number of items in the system, this is reflected in the above definition showing the difference between an individual item compared with larger quantities in the complete system.

The Designer and WPA need to make the risk assessment using their detailed knowledge of the item concerned, they should not consider the cost implications or worry about the level of risk if it is not at an acceptable level initially. The assessment must be a true value made by an expert in that domain.

The ultimate aim is to reduce the risk level to the lowest possible point. This is achieved by implementing preventative measures and actions.

At the start of a project it is often the case that the information available is limited and the design is still very crude however the basic plans are usually known, for example it will be known if electricity, pressure, or masts are going to be used. A Hazard List can be generated followed by a Preliminary Hazard Analysis.

The Hazard Analysis will slowly be produced as the detailed design takes shape and each WPA has a defined knowledge of all the components and the hazards they contain.

One of the best ways to document a hazard and the associated risk is by generating a series of Hazard Logs that can be compiled and placed into a ring binder entitled the Hazard Analysis. The best person to collect and compile the logs presented by each Work Package Area is the Project Safety Engineer.

The Safety Engineer must check that the information contained in the log makes sense and the risk assessment is acceptable and where not acceptable, actions and corrective measures have been specified.

Each hazard must have a hazard log sheet and the log is allocated a serial number for tracking purposes

A description of the hazard should be written in clear and defined terms, so that persons who do not have a detailed knowledge of the item can understand the hazard. There will be the designers risk assessment plus the danger or consequence.

The log will show in detail the recommended corrective measures to be taken. Once the corrective actions have been implemented the residual risk assessment is inserted this will show the risk is at an acceptable level in accordance with the Hazard Risk Assessment in the cases where the risks cannot be reduced to an acceptable level following corrective measures the log cannot be closed.

A log shall only be closed following a signature by the appropriate Safety Authority

An example of a typical Hazard Log is shown overleaf

Hazard Log Sheet

Reference Number: *001 Instrumentation*   **Date Raised:** *01.08.12*
Item Name: *Automatic Unit (Car Window)*

Description of Hazard: *The closing of all car windows are activated remotely by the car driver away from the rear window location.*

Cause and Consequence: *Severe injury or death to other car occupants such as children and pets that may have their head or other parts of the body over the window sill at the time.*

Hazard Risk Index: **Category:** *1*   **Level:** *B*

**Recommended
Action to be Taken:**   *a) Design change to alter automatic window closure to Manual system with low climb rate.*

b) Incorporate pressure switch to automatic system. Obstruction to activate the reverse command to the windows from upward to down ward.

Action Actually Taken: *Design change to manual system in accordance with (a) above.*

Residual Hazard Risk Index: **Category:** *1* **Level:** *E*

Close out Signatures: **Date:**
Auditor

Project Manager

Chapter 5
Hazard Operability Studies (HAZOP)

Many years ago the Chemical Industry found a need to devise a unique way of monitoring which is known as Hazard Operability Studies that has been shortened to HAZOP.

This method of safety has been expanded in recent years and is now used throughout industry and is particularly suitable for the safety of software.

We tend to believe that a system or process will always operate correctly as it was designed, the HAZOP method questions this and basically asks the question What are the consequences if a component or process fails to work? What if!

In the case of software we may have a processor with several inputs and outputs on which we are sending command messages or trigger messages to operate our system.

Our intention is to send and receive from a to b on these links. What would happen if these messages became corrupted or failed to reach their destination? There may be no affect to the system at all but what if the data was a piece of vital information used on medical equipment or a message to arm an anti missile missile.

Alternatively there could be a high pressure system of gas or liquid and what would be the consequences if a pressure release valve failed to operate?

The HAZOP system is an analytical technique that uses a process of imagination, experience and deduction by experts to identify potential accidents. The HAZOP process is particularly suitable for the analysis of software systems and Sub-system and System levels in hardware.

A team of experts in the relevant domain are assembled together and are provided with a context diagram or flow chart of the equipment or process being analysed.

The study leader should then involve all of the team members in generating possible deviations from the intended process of operation and establish the cause and consequence of the deviation from the intention.

The team are guided by considering the definitions listed below, plus a set of Guide Words. The deviation from the intended operation is then converted into a hazard that is associated with the Cause and Consequence. The final stage is to conduct a Hazard Risk Assessment to ascertain the severity and probability of occurrence.

Intention:	How the part is expected to operate (Use flow chart(s) or Context Diagram)
Deviation:	Departures from the *Intention* which are discovered by systematically applying the guide words.
Cause:	The reasons why *Deviations* might occur. Once a *Deviation* has been shown to have a conceivable or realistic cause it can be treated as meaningful.
Consequence:	The results of *Deviations* should they occur.
Hazards:	*Consequences* which can cause damage, injury, or loss.
Guide Words:	Simple words used to quantify the *Intention* to guide and stimulate the creative thinking process and show the *Deviations* that can occur.

It should be noted that the following list of Guide Words do not have to be used in the HAZOP analysis as long as the same results are achieved.

Guide Word	Meaning	Comments
NOTHING	The complete negation of the intention.	No part of the intention is achieved but nothing else occurs.
MORE	Quantitative increase	In quantities or actions associated with the intention.

LESS	Quantitative decrease	In quantities or actions associated with the intention.
AS WELL AS	Quantitative increase, plus something extra.	All the intentions are achieved together with some additional activity.
PART OF	Quantitative decrease intention is not completed	Only some of the intentions are achieved some are not..
REVERSE	The opposite of the intention.	The reverse of the intended action occurs.
OTHER THAN	Complete substitution	No part of the intention is achieved something different happens.

So if we were to ask our experts to apply these rules to a software link between two processors they should discover the hazards.

Processor A------------------------*Message*------------------------**Processor B**

The **Intention** is to send our message from Processor A to Processor B
What would happen if the message was not sent?
What would happen if the message had too many characters?
What would happen if the message had too few characters?
These are some **Deviations** from what we expect to happen and our experts job is to establish what the **Consequences** are and list the **Hazards plus the Risk levels.**

Process Design Plan
Stage 2

<u>Design Reviews.</u>

Safety shall always be on the agenda of Design Reviews It is vital that the reviews are attended by the relevant people and should be postponed until everyone is available. The following persons should be present as a minimum

The Designer
The Design Authority
A Quality Engineer
A Safety Engineer

The safety information presented should be the latest available Hazard logs that relate to the equipment being discussed, all attendees should be provided with a copy. The information contained in the logs shall be reviewed and any additions noted for document update. These logs are going to form the data contained in the Hazard Analysis raised for every item of equipment in the system. It should be remembered that in large projects the Hazard Analysis can extend into many volumes.

One of the aims of the meeting is to ensure that the Hazards are at an acceptable level with regard to risk. In the situation where large changes are required to make an item safe the data shall be passed to higher management for a decision that may entail further funding.

All Hazard Risk Index(s) (HRI(s) shall be at an acceptable level in accordance with the Hazard Assessment Chart before the product is traded.

Project Managers can receive regular safety information on the current Risk levels by the use of a specially adapted Hazard Risk Assessment Chart. Safety presenters can show hazards that require corrective measures by placing Hazard Log Reference Numbers onto a Hazard Risk Assessment Chart please see example below.

Catastrophic	Critical	Marginal	Negligible
Frequent	150	*serial number of*	
		hazard log sheet	
Probable	007, 045,		

Occasional		**024, 029,**	**036**
Remote	**114, 205,**	**111, 158,**	
Improbable	**200,**	**140,116,**	

Process Design Plan
Stage 3

Commercial Off The Shelf (COTS) Equipment.

Following the dramatic decline of manufactured goods in the United Kingdom many companies have resorted to `buying in` components and incorporating them into their systems. In some cases they have to be modified to meet the requirements of the system that can invalidate the warranty of the original manufacturer.

COTS can be a headache for the safety personnel because they are often produced overseas and arrive with little or no safety data. In many situations the component may be in the form of a sealed unit, the other problem is that sometimes these units are being placed in environmental conditions for which they were not designed.

It really does not make much sense to make a system safe by completing a detailed hazard analysis and then introduce a COTS item for which nothing is known.

Ensure that before COTS items are purchased the supplier provides all of the relevant safety information because once you accept the component and place into your system you are accountable if anyone is harmed. It would almost be impossible to prove liability with regard to the COTS supplier.

When COTS items are present it is essential that a comprehensive and sustained Design Proving Programme is carried out.

Those Companies providing equipment for the military should check with the customer before using any COTS item to ensure that the commercial build meets the Military standards in the Requirements.

Chapter 6

Stage 4

Audit Reports

When the design and development process is coming to a conclusion in other words a finished prototype is in place and any further changes are unlikely an Audit is carried out.

Audits are completed on every piece of equipment plus their needs to be a further top level audit once all of the equipment is connected together in a system.

The Auditor should if possible come from a different project the reason for this is to obtain a completely different approach from those working closely with the design.

To help the Auditor to become familiar with the safety problems already identified he shall be provided with a copy of the Hazard Analysis (Safety Logs). He is to go to each equipment and systematically go through every log sheet and ensure that the Action taken statement has been completed to his or her satisfaction. He or she will also be required to look at the equipment from an independent viewpoint to ascertain if anything has been overlooked or needs to be added with regard to safety.

Once the Auditor is satisfied with the precautions that have been implemented a signature is placed at the bottom of each Hazard log. In the situations where the Auditor requires additional action(s) another Hazard Log is raised and passed back to the design team to implement. The Auditor has to be satisfied with the subsequent corrective action before the equipment can be released.

The Audit Report should contain a complete list of the all the units and components audited plus any comments that are appropriate. Any changes to the equipment should have an Engineering Change Request form that provides all the evidence that corrective measures have been taken, the Audit Report needs to reference these also.

The structured process has now produced a comprehensive list of documentation that can be presented to show that the system or process has been examined to identify and reduce the risk of any safety hazards and therefore establish the System/Process is inherently safe.

System Safety Programme Plan
Hazard List
Preliminary Hazard Analysis
Hazard Analysis
Hazard Operability Study
Safety Audit

SECTION 8
Product Item Equipment Configurations.

Built in Test and Built in Test Equipment BIT/ BITE.

When designing large systems or processes it is important that consideration is given to when it develops a fault and ensure it is detected and corrected as soon as possible.

It is in every ones interest to keep systems running without too much disruption a computer failure as we all know can cause major disruption to anything from a Super Market to the Air Traffic Control System.

If some provision is not made in the design for fault detection in equipment, and strings of components are placed into a system when it fails finding the fault can be like looking for a needle in a haystack

It is not easy to decide how sophisticated to make fault detection but once the decision is made all the main equipment should have the same level and cost needs to be allocated accordingly.

There are vital systems that run two strings of equipment and if one fails the second one on hot standby will take over, however it is not always the case that one can afford this level of sophistication. One other method is that a fault indication is given on a Line Replaceable Unit and the faulty equipment is withdrawn and replaced, this again can be an expensive option due to the duplication of large units.

The flagging of a fault down to a small component also has its problems because of the test equipment needed and the detailed design required to pin point the faulty component.

It is not uncommon to reconfigure a system around the area that is causing the problem. When this occurs safety precautions need to be in place that leave all those concerned in no doubt what configuration the system is in and which parts of the system are active, following reconfiguration.

One of the most common methods used is to take equipment that have faults off line this should prevent unnecessary fault messages being generated.

One of the main safety implications involved when equipment is under maintenance is other personnel can be injured due to confusion on what is in use and what is not also equipment unexpectedly being placed back into use without warning.

Chapter 7
Responsibilities for Hazard Analysis

In the high tech society of today we often see not just one company involved in the generation of a product but several, so it is very important that if we are to ensure safety is adequately covered each of the companies must know what they need to analyse and where the boundaries are and when it is someone else who is responsible.

To ensure all companies know what is expected of them the Prime contractor shall provide clear Safety Requirements and set in place good lines of communication directly into the controlling company.

There have been quite a number of communication and liaison problems in the past one being the Airborne Early Warning Aircraft Nimrod contract where the Aircraft was not compatible with the equipment that needed to go into it.

More recently a Shipyard in the north of England built a number of military ships for an overseas navy and most of the guns and electronic equipment was subcontracted out to specialist companies. One of the specialist companies designed and made a sophisticated piece of electronic equipment that was housed below decks. The equipment when working had lethal thousands of volts passing through it that needed to be adjusted to be at a precise setting. The setting up process required the engineer to make the adjustment using a insulated tool and a meter, to complete this task a pair of cabinet doors were opened and the equipment pulled out on runners and locked into place. The company producing the equipment specified the minimum amount of space required in front of the equipment to complete the operation safety.

The ship was built and the equipment installed however it was then discovered the space required had been ignored and only a portion was available, this resulted in once the cabinet doors were open there was no room for the engineer to pass around them. The worst part was that the setting up of the lethal voltage would have to be completed from the side of the equipment using a raised step up or ladder. The other implications of all this were the maintenance manual had been written outlining the setting up procedure using the original space required. This left equipment manufacturer with a dilemma if the handbook was not changed the maintainer would be left to his own devices because the written procedures were not possible to complete, however to change the procedure could result in an poor safety accusation. The moral of this is that a lack of communication and safety requirements has produced a situation for which there is no easy answer. If a maintainer were to come to harm who would be held responsible the shipbuilder, or the electronic company who have had to compromised their preferred safety by having to decide whether to rewrite the setting up procedures to accommodate the lack of space?

The System Safety Programme Plan shall show who has overall responsibility for the safety of each area and the lines of communication

COMPLETED SYSTEMS AND EQUIPMENT.

Legacy Equipment.

This guide has considered the structured process involved when designing safety into equipment during design and development, however there maybe a requirement to complete a Hazard Analysis on an already built system or what we will term as Legacy Equipment.

It is not impossible to achieve but far less comprehensive than the safety analysis completed in the design phase of current equipment. The first problem is knowing what hazards are contained in each component, it is not feasible to strip down equipment to try and analyse what they are made up of and normally the designers have moved on.

However it is advantageous to complete a limited analysis rather than do nothing

Our structured process of System Safety Plan, Hazard Analysis, Risk Assessment, HAZOP and Audit should still be used in these situations but conducted on the external areas of the system only. In some circumstances you may be lucky and have some drawings to help.

Equipment returned for repair or refurbishment should be subjected to safety analysis but the cost of any major changes can be a problem.

Companies have a responsibility to ensure the public come to no harm from the products placed on the market and even though they have incorporated safety measures, unless they have documented evidence to prove it, they leave themselves in a weak position in any litigation brought against them .

To prevent unsafe products from leaving the company the company safety directorate should sign a release certificate following proof of a full set of safety documents being presented and reviewed.

In situations where legacy equipment is involved full Design Safety Certification cannot be signed due to the limited nature of the analysis.

Incident Reports.
A customer may report an incident with regard to equipment that has been in the field for some years. All Incident Reports must be thoroughly checked and responded to and if it is found that there is a safety risk a Safety Alert is raised and a Hazard Analysis shall be initiated and corrective measures generated.

Safety Alerts
A Safety Alert shall be initiated and passed to all customers who have taken delivery of the same equipment.

Chapter 8
Human Factors Engineering (HFE)

Human Factors Engineering needs to be implemented in the design of all products. It is unfortunate that not enough attention is given in this area and as a consequence this leads to problems in maintenance and normal operation.

Most of us have experienced HFE problems in every day tasks such as changing components needing repair and having a problem reaching the faulty item.

Anyone who has driven a strange car for the first time knows how difficult it can be in the first few minutes to become familiar with the instrumentation positions and how easy it is to operate the wipers instead of the indicators.

A lack of Human Factors Engineering can result in dangerous situations for example if the placing of a sign on the motorway fails to provide sufficient warning of a hazard or information there is a high chance it could result in an accident.

There needs to be forward planning in some situations such as the delivery of a heavy item to a location and ensuring it can be safety off loaded. The customer and the supplier can so easily assume that the other has taken care of everything.

The correct control of the environment is vital for staff to complete their tasks safety . If personnel are too hot, too cold, given insufficient light or exposed to severe noise it can lead to a decrease in efficiency, concentration, alertness and cause permanent injury and illness.

Many accidents are caused by a lack of concentration or tiredness.

The safety analysis should always include the Human Factors Engineering element

The two main areas must include a System Analysis and a Critical Task Analysis

The HFE System Analysis involves the description of the system layout plus the working methods and procedures. The information will contain the number of personnel maintaining a system and what facilities and methods they employ to complete their responsibilities.

The HFE Critical Task Analysis tracks the person and specifies all of his/her actions and body movements for the completion of a task from beginning to end.

Let us pretend that we have a control room that contains monitoring equipment and is manned by staff for twenty four hours a day

Before we analyse anything we have to identify all of the tasks that have to be completed.

Is the room entrance level with the floor outside? Yes / No

If 'No' how is faulty equipment removed and installed?

What are the maximum number of staff that can be employed in the room at one time?

Where are the emergency exits and how do staff use them?

Can personnel cope with the workload on each position?

How long can each person spend on each position ?

Once all of these types of questions have been listed each task can be analysed to ascertain what measures are required to complete the task in a safe manner.

Human Factors will provide the correct aperture, clearance, spacing, height weight, light intensity, etc and will provide information that relates to anthropometric data. In other words it allows for the fact that we are not all of the same stature, or gender.

If a company is designing an escape hatchway it is vital that even the largest person can pass through it. .

When staff are sat at desks and workstations for hours a day it is important that their posture is considered. If they are sat at the wrong angle or their chair is at the incorrect height it can lead to a number of illnesses such as back strain, circulation problems and repetitive strain syndrome.

Human Factors must also be considered with regard to maintenance. If a component fails the maintainer should not have to take apart most of the equipment to reach it.

System Safety Programme Plan.
Section 9
Attachments
(The Attachments in this example are those that could be found in a Safety Occupational Health Document.)

Example
Cadmium Solders and Plated Metals.
Cadmium shall not be used.

Cadmium is a silver-white lustrous metal that tarnishes in air It has various uses and those more likely to be encountered are as a constituent of some hard solders or as material electroplated on other metals to reduce the effects of corrosion.

Cadmium plating applied to other metals especially fixings made of mild and stainless steel are treated to provide more resistance against corrosion and can be recognised by a yellow or multi coloured appearance.

Under normal circumstances the handling of this coating presents no hazard however if corrosion of the cadmium plate does take place the powdery white substance that is formed (cadmium hydroxide commonly described as white rust) is highly toxic

Cadmium has a relatively low melting point and if slightly overheated, molten cadmium is easily ignited and burns giving off copious amounts of brown smoke consisting of cadmium oxide. This smoke is extremely toxic.

The health hazard arises by the inhalation of cadmium dust of fume or by ingestion of its compounds. This can give rise to symptoms of acute poisoning after a brief exposure to a high concentration or of chronic poisoning after prolonged exposure to a smaller concentration.

Any person suffering even minor symptoms of cadmium poisoning must be referred to medical personnel.

Beryllium Oxide (Beryllia).
Parts or components containing sintered Beryllium Oxide or Beryllia for short can present a health hazard unless adequate precautions are taken.

The hazard comes from dust. Beryllia is very hard and although slight abrasion does not normally cause dust, if a part is roughly handled or broken dust maybe created.

A secondary hazard can be caused by overheating such as welding.

The health risk are particles penetrating the skin through cuts, wounds or abrasions and may be difficult to heal.

Inhalation or ingestion of small quantities of dust over long periods can be as injurious to health as a single acute exposure.

Symptoms of poisoning are respiratory troubles or cyanosis (grey blue dis-colouration of the skin) may develop within a week or even after a latent period of several years.

System Safety Programme Plan.
Section 10
Design Approval and Design Certification.

How can the staff in corporate management be sure that the company has satisfied all of the requirements with regard to the Design and the Safety of a product?

The best way to ensure a product has met all of the requirements is to obtain as much evidence as possible, this is easier said than done because to be presented with a mass of documents would confuse the situation even more. However if the evidence is in the form of a signature placed on a Design Approval Form that contained a list of key Design Authorities it makes things more manageable. Each Authority must be satisfied the design and safety are at an acceptable level The Safety Authority will add his or her signature after he/she is satisfied the structured process has been completed and the relevant documents are all in place. These documents will include at least the following

The System Safety Programme Plan
The Hazard Analysis
The Hazard and Operability Study
The Audit Report (with no outstanding Hazard Log Sheets)

The Directorate is then asked to sign a Design Certification Certificate for the release of the product onto the open market, providing they are satisfied everything is in order.

The directors concerned are supplied with the following evidence by all the Design Authorities at a short meeting where any questions can be answered

The Safety Documents listed above.

The Design Approval Form containing all of the Signatures of the Authorities plus the Project Manager.

Section 10 of the Programme Plan should contain a blank copy of the Design Approval form and Design Certification Certificate with an explanation of the procedure for obtaining product clearance.

This concludes all of the contents recommended for the System Safety programme Plan.

Chapter 9
Safety Integrity Levels

Even though each part of the system has been analysed and assessed it is vital that we assess the system as a complete entity. We could have incorporated some functionality that is completely dependant on software. We therefore have to consider what the software is doing and if there is an automatic software process for which we have no direct influence on in real time. Let us say for example we are testing rockets If we are about fire a rocket using manual inputs and there is a problem it should be possible to intervene and stop the launch, however if we have only used an automated system we could find ourselves in a sequence of events that is difficult to abort.

When we use Safety Integrity Levels the same terminology is used as previously stated in the Risk Assessment i.e. Catastrophic, Critical, Marginal, Negligible for severity and Frequent, Probable Occasional, Remote, Improbable for probability.

However in the previous scale the most severe state was level 1 where as here it is the lowest level and the most severe is Level S4 which includes Catastrophic and Critical, Marginal at Level S3 and Negligible Level S2. The term SIL is commonly used when Integrity Levels are being discussed.

Following Analysis if it is found that there is a SIL Level of S4 there is a good chance Safety Critical Software is present in the system.

When Safety Critical Software is used a set of rules must be implemented that includes backup and monitoring processes. This is a specialist subject beyond the scope of this guide and if further information is required any good software house will provide assistance.

Hazard List.
Preliminary Hazard Analysis.

Following the completion of the System Safety Programme Plan the generation of a Hazard List and Preliminary Hazard Analysis should be started this will give the Management a good indication on which areas the main safety shall be focussed early in the project life cycle.

As an example let us pretend we are a company that provides floodlighting and an order has been received from the Far East that requires a race course used for horse racing to be floodlit for night race meetings.

Even though we do not have the requirements yet we can still initiate a Hazard List on the things we know that will require safety inputs and the implications.

Hazard List.
Masts
Corrosion
Typhoons
Obstruction and location of masts
Unauthorised climbing
Subsidence
Flood light positioning
Electrical power
Maintenance
Flooding by monsoon rain
Power Failure

Of course this list would be generated by the design teams (WPA) in normal circumstances who should also use the Primary and Secondary Check Lists in Chapter 3 Section 7

Preliminary Hazard Analysis.
The Hazard List can be expanded into the Preliminary Hazard Analysis where we raise a number of Hazard Log Sheets in relation to the Hazard List and assess the risk of each hazard and recommend corrective action where possible. The information can be very patchy at this early stage of the contract but it will provide an excellent starting point. This data can be used in discussions with the customer on the initial visit to survey the site.

Final Hazard Analysis.
This is one of the main safety documents and will contain all of the Hazard Log Sheets that have been generated by the Designers in each Work Package Area. The customer requirements should have now been defined and the data contained in the Preliminary Hazard Analysis flowed into this document. As the design progresses and develops the Hazard Log Sheets are updated until the lowest possible acceptable risk is achieved.

The Project Safety Engineer should provide every Work Package Area with a set of paper work that includes an extract of the System Safety Programme Plan that explains the methodology, a list of Check Lists, and Blank Hazard Log Sheet for Photo Copying. If this information can be installed electronically on the companies internal website it will enhance the process.

All data should be returned to the Project Safety Engineer who will review and collate the Hazard Log Sheets into the Final Hazard Analysis and insert the next Hazard sheet reference number in the sequence. Due to the number of hazard log sheets that are contained in a Hazard Analysis the Document needs to be divided up into logical sections that pertain to the different parts of the system.

Audit Report.

The Auditor is the person carrying out the final safety check and if possible would have not been involved with any reviews or analyses of the equipment or system being audited.

Before the audit takes place the equipment or system must be complete, being the final version. The auditor will take a copy of the Final Hazard Analysis and check that the action on each Hazard Log sheet has been completed. It is a good idea to provide a project member of staff who is familiar with the system to help the auditor because he or she will know which location the component is in and in some, dismantling may be involved. If machinery or electrical equipment is being audited the equipment should be placed on line in order that the emergency power off and circuit breakers can be tested.

The report should show the date, those present, and a list of the equipment that was audited. The auditor must show a list of the Hazard Log Sheet Numbers that have been verified and comment on any outstanding observations.

It is also the Auditors task to assess the design from an independent viewpoint and comment on anything that has been overlooked or needs addressing.

Chapter 10
CE Marking

Why do we need it?

CE Relates to European Conformity.

It is an offence within the European Community to offer for sale or supply products without a CE mark. The CE mark is the manufacturers declaration that the product conforms in all respects with the essential requirements of the appropriate EC Directives.

The areas concerned include all European Union Member States plus EFTA (European Free trade Association) Member States that include but may not limited to Iceland, Liechtenstein, and Norway.

The CE Mark has been created to aid the smooth passing of goods across borders of different European Countries and to enhance trade. There are a great assortment of different standards which differ from one area to another and once the cross border restrictions were relaxed it was imperative that a harmonisation of standards took place. A series of European Directives have been produced to provide guidance on what is required. A product must be analysed to ascertain what it contains this will provide what Directives are appropriate. There are different Directives that cover Machinery, Electrical, Pressure Vessels, EMC, etc.

Before a CE Mark can be attached, the product shall conform to all of the appropriate directives and have the documentation to prove it and this has to be available for at least ten years, the CE Mark in its self is basically there only to assist Customs staff.

Once a company adopts a structured safety process as described in this guide it will help with the compliance for CE Marking due to the creation of a Technical File and a Hazard Analysis.

The Directives set out `attestation` procedures for assessing whether a product conforms with the essential requirements.

Chapter 11
Conclusions and Consolidation

At the beginning of this guide it was stated that nothing is one hundred percent safe so we will always have accidents in one form or another. We often see that one small problem will develop into a string of events that can result into a catastrophic disaster such as the Air France Concorde crash in Paris. One piece of metal on the runway set in motion a string of events when the tyre burst and the fragments punctured the fuel tank which then became ignited. So what can be done to try and reduce these situations occurring in everyday life? The answer is to introduce a safety culture into everything we put in place, this does not mean a nanny state policy it means a common Structured Safety Policy throughout business and industry.

Everyone in business should ask themselves this question Would our products processes, or procedures stand up to close safety scrutiny with regard to providing proof and evidence of Hazard Analysis and Acceptable Risk.?

The clock is ticking and tighter safety legislation is imminent which means that any organisation that fails to meet the safety commitment will be accountable.

As a final exercise and help consolidate the different elements discussed in this guide we shall assume that we have been given the task of introducing a safety culture into a Railway Network

We have a country wide system that has one company who is responsible for the infrastructure i.e the lines, overhead power, and stations, etc and over twenty operating companies who run the trains.

The first thing we have to ensure is the lines of communication between all of these companies and introduce a direct reporting structure that is simple to use and easily monitored. One company must be made responsible for the safety organisation of the network, this is not a difficult choice because the obvious candidate is the infrastructure company. This company has two major roles one as an overseer of the train operating companies and the other putting in place its own safety organisation.

A team of trained Safety Engineers shall be appointed , at least one for each company. One system shall be agreed by all companies to ensure everyone is singing from the same hymn sheet. A System Safety Programme Plan needs to be written for the Network that shows communication paths through each layer of management, there also needs to be a clear directive to all the operating companies on what documentation (Tasks) need to be generated with copies supplied to the controlling company. The operating companies must not be left to their own devices and shall use the processes and methodology specified in the System Safety Programme Plan.

Remember the Plan must clearly spell out where the boundaries of responsibility are so there are no gaps in the safety analyses.

The first task is to divide the network into logical chunks, the top level can be twenty plus units which make up the operating companies. We can take each one of these companies and divide them into the number of routes that they control. Each route is then split into sections, of about twenty miles.

Each operating company is required to provide a set of safety documents that is in accordance with the System Safety Programme Plan for each route it operates.

There needs to be information that covers all aspects of the route that may present hazards, this includes the infrastructure for that the train operator is not responsible.

We need to know the route in detail this is achieved by completing a Human Factors Engineering System Analysis. Our system is a Legacy system in other words it already exists so all we have to do is travel backwards forwards on the train with the driver until each section is mapped out along the complete route.

The HFE System Analysis provides a written description such as the train departure station is a single platform on the left side of the train and the line terminates with a set of buffers. The train power is supplied by an overhead electrical line supported by gantries. When the train departs the station the line bends to the right and crosses over a road bridge the line then snakes to the left and passes over the second road bridge at approximately three miles station two is on the left hand side. The line passes between two forty feet high banks on either side and so on. The analyses gives details of signals, level crossings, stations and tunnels all the way along the route. Which is then enhanced by a drawn map. The insertion of digital photographs of the key features can also be included.

The next task is to group the staff into logical Work Package Areas (WPAs) that could include the following

Station Staff
Signalmen
Track Maintenance Staff
Overhead Power and Electrical Crews
Civil Engineers
Drivers and Guards

Each group is then briefed on the methodology used to conduct a Hazard Analysis and Risk Assessment. This training is the job of the area Safety Engineer he is the person who will organise, review and compile the completed data.

The HFE System Analysis is given to the WPAs associated with the infrastructure and each group is asked to provide a Hazard Analysis of each section of the route, including the recommended speed limits over bridges and restricted zones.

The Station Staff need to provide a set of rules and procedures to prevent accidents plus conduct a Hazard Analysis. Contractors have been killed on stations in the past by placing long metal objects such as scaffold too close to the power lines while carrying them along the platform

The Train Drivers are required to provide a Human Factors Engineering Critical Task Analysis this gives details of the drivers actions while driving the route it will include speed changes and signal reading. The information obtained from the HFE System Analysis will be input into this document and can be used as a training aid in the classroom for new drivers. It will show signal locations speed restrictions and other relevant data.

We are told that train drivers sometimes pass through red lights SPADs Signals passed at Danger. One can only assume that this action is not done on purpose so is there a lack of concentration or some other reason? Do we expect too much of the Train Driver of today who is travelling at speeds up to one hundred and twenty miles an hour on congested routes in rain, bright sunshine, mist etc with hundreds of passengers? Why is only one person considered adequate?

with AUTOMATIC Train Protection it may be sufficient. An in depth Hazard Analysis should answer all of these questions.

The data from each Work Package Area is all collected by the area Safety Engineer and each of the Hazard Log Sheets is given a reference number and placed into a series of ring binders entitled Safety Hazard Analysis Route—Section 1-2-3-4

It is vital that the corrective action on the Hazard Log Sheets is implemented and in this case some of the recommended actions may not have been written by the originator of the Hazard Log. A train driver may have raised a Hazard Log stating that a particular signal was difficult to read, however he works for the operating company who have no responsibility for the infrastructure so the Safety Engineer would send this to the appropriate area for action following review.

To enable the moving of the signal an Engineering Change Request must be raised and providing the Configuration Control staff of the infrastructure company agree the work is carried out. They must justify in a written report if the Engineering Request is rejected for any reason. Because this involves safety there would have to be a very good reason if the change is rejected. The originator of the Hazard Log should be given a copy of the report so that he can see why it was rejected and allow for appeal.

The Safety Engineer needs to frequently review the Hazard Analysis and track the progress of the Hazard Log actions. Once he is informed the work has been completed he will then make arrangements for a qualified person to complete an Audit and supply the Auditor with a copy of the Hazard Log and a Engineering Change Request form where applicable.

There will be a point in time where every Company will have a Hazard Analysis for every route that it controls and it only remains for the update of the binders when a change is carried out, or a member of staff inputs a new Hazard Log Sheet.

We have dealt with the legacy equipment and the safety organisation associated with the design and development of new rolling stock has been explained earlier.

It has been stated that we have to consider hazards that were inconceivable in the past such as what occurred at the Twin Towers in New York on the 11th of September, 2001.and the case of the Metropolitan Police in London who were involved in the tragic shooting of an innocent person at Stockwell Underground

Station. The police were on a high state of alert following a number of terrorist bombs in London.

A Portuguese immigrant was wrongly identified and shot dead on an Underground train.

In this case the Safety Act should have been a fundamental part of their procedures. To ensure this does not happen again. How could safety be incorporated by using Hazard Analysis and Risk Assessment in the future?

If we consider Severity there could be an assessment (possible explosive belt or bag) assuming the worst case that the suspect has a device on his person. If he detonated it in a highly populated street it would be **Catastrophic** (1 in our chart) or if he was in empty street it could be **Critical** (2 in our chart) or on the outskirts of town **Marginal** (3 in our chart) At a remote deserted farmhouse we would have a level 4 **Negligible.** However because the suspect is moving the situation is *dynamic* and could change in a short space of time.

The other part of our analyses is the Probability, remember there are five levels A to E This assessment is crucial because it will indicate how certain we are about the suspects identity. If we are 99% sure that the suspect is a terrorist, level (A) on our chart then there is a high probability and our Hazard Risk Index levels should acted on. However if there is doubt about whom our suspect is 50% to 60% probability B on our chart then this is going to affect the Probability due to the fact that the suspect is less likely to have a device. So if there is a course of action associated with each level of Hazard Risk Index it will greatly enhance the senior police officers task on when to take action.

The methods described in this guide have been used to provide a comprehensive system of safety over many years and if implemented by the readers will provide them with a safety culture for the future.

Reference Publications

System Safety Program Requirements	Mil Std 882
Standard	Def Std 0056
Human Factors Engineering	Mil Std 1472
Human Factors Engineering	Def Std 0025
Hazard Operability Study	Def Std 0058

Index

Training Programme.

This guide has been designed to be used as a training tool and allows for safety personnel to easily prepare a Safety Training Package. The key facts can be extracted from the main body of the text and produced on presentation material.

It is recommended that the training should be divided into six main parts

Safety Awareness,
Methodology of Hazard Analysis and Risk Assessment,
Auditing,
Hazard Operability Studies,
Human Factors Engineering,
CE Marking.

THE AUTHOR

The author has many years experience of managing safety systems. This includes the role of Safety and Human Factors Engineer for a multi million pound over the horizon radar project for the Australian Department of Defence.

He has also held the position of the Product Safety Assurance Authority for a multi national company with six hundred products in forty countries.